Colorado

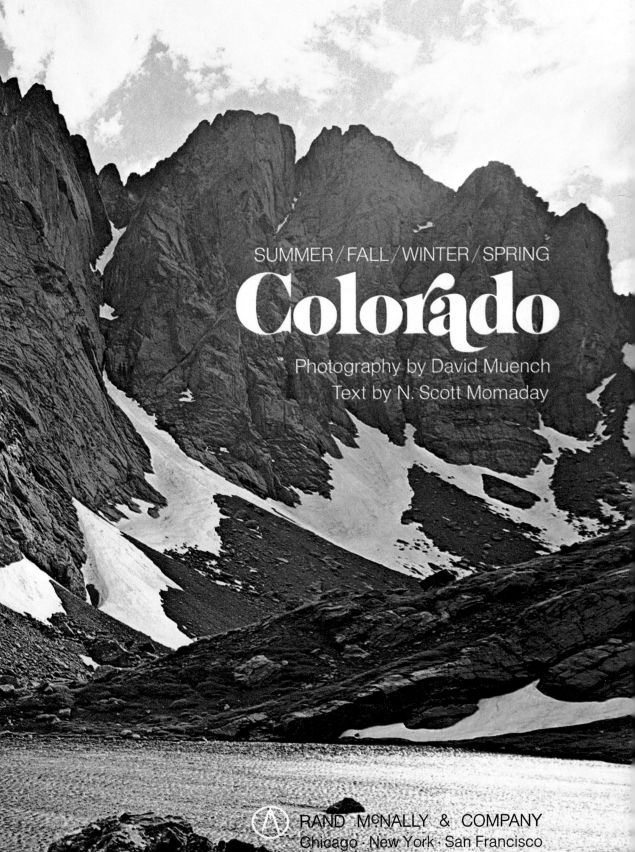

SUMMER / FALL / WINTER / SPRING

Colorado

Photography by David Muench

Text by N. Scott Momaday

Ⓐ RAND McNALLY & COMPANY
Chicago · New York · San Francisco

◄ Sangre de Cristo Range

Colorado State Flag

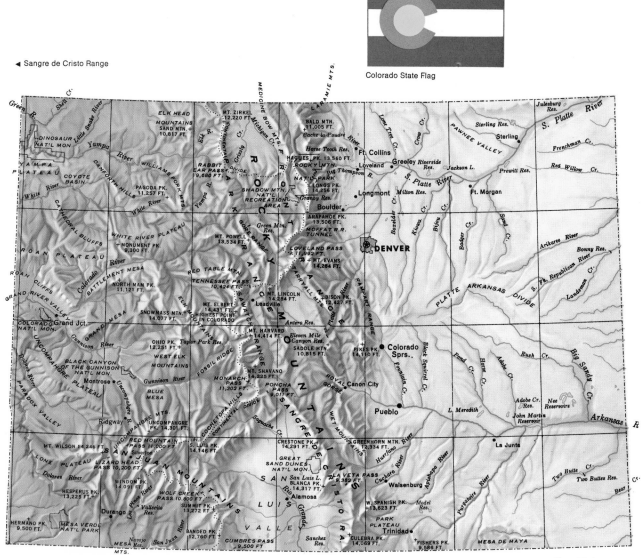

Map of Colorado

Book Design by MARIO PAGLIAI

Copyright © 1973 by RAND McNALLY & COMPANY
All Rights Reserved
Library of Congress Catalog Card Number: 73-4956
ISBN: 0-528-81909-7
Printed in the United States of America
by RAND McNALLY & COMPANY

Third printing, 1978

Contents

Colorado

MY MIND has been involved in the landscape of Colorado for a long time—from the moment I was old enough to conceive an idea of my homeland (I have lived most of my life in view of the Rocky Mountains); my blood even longer. For my ancestors were native to the highlands of the continent. They were the *Gaigwu* (Kiowa), the "coming out" people, who believed that they had entered the world through a hollow log. That was far to the north, near the headwaters of the Yellowstone River. Three hundred years ago, more or less, the Kiowa moved down from their origin place. They began a long journey to the south and east, coming at last to the place of their destiny in the southern plains. On their way, through the long rain shadow of the Rockies, they inhabited the eastern slope of what is now Colorado.

Gore Range from Williams Fork Mountains

Time and again I have entered into that landscape, taken possession of it in my imagination, given myself up to it. It is vast and irregular, the most emphatic geology in North America; so I think of it. There is no end to it, but it is indivisible with the whole earth and sky. In a sense "Colorado" is the name of the continent, elevated to its full height. The rectangle that one observes on a map—and there only—is an intelligent fiction, and it bears no real relation to the land, at last. In spite of man's relentless efforts to impose the patterns of his mind upon the earth, yet he encounters a wild, organic resistance, a wilderness that geometry does not comprehend. In Colorado, high upon the spine of North America, one has a keen sense of the original earth, of its deep, definitive life. At Cripple Creek, in September, I think: Nothing is so exhilarating as this, to stand just here on the rim of the plain, at midmorning, and feel the world's turning—the slow, persistent spinning of the planet in its universe.

Trout Lake, San Juan Mountains

At La Junta—or Leadville or Creede—I am reminded
of Colorado history, which is the story of man in this particular
landscape. It is a brief story, relatively. Man is especially here
a newcomer, even as this western wilderness is especially the
New World—and yet the skyline, in all directions, is the very
image of geologic time; the contrast is striking. And yet it is a
whole story, too, intricate in motion and design.

The earliest evidence of man in Colorado suggests a
gradual infiltration of the eastern slope at the end of the last
Ice Age. Certain stone artifacts found there, the so-called
Folsom and Yuma points in particular, which appear to
represent two separate but contemporaneous cultures, are
thought by some archaeologists to be 20,000 years old or
older. Of these Stone Age men we know very little, indeed: that
they were hunters, that they were constantly engaged in a
struggle to survive, and that they were remarkably skillful
in shaping stone to their use.

In the peneplain, where at times I have seen glittering
snowfields on the mountainsides in the distance, and so have
had a sense of the Ice Age in retreat, I have imagined a man
of that race, a dark and shaggy figure, set deep into the field of
my vision like a brier, the setting sun fixing a luster upon him;
and in his hand a faceted weapon or a tool, delicate, deftly
fashioned—a thing that bears the human trace. What
became of him?

Not until the time of Christ did another people appear in Colorado, persist in isolation for a time, and pass from the scene, leaving innumerable signs of their coming and going. These were the Basket Makers of the San Juan basin. Their sedentary and agricultural society was appropriated, as it were, by the succeeding Pueblo culture, which came to full flower about the year 1000. The great prehistoric architecture of Mesa Verde dates from this period.

At the end of the thirteenth century the Pueblo culture came to an end in Colorado, perhaps because of a severe and prolonged drought, perhaps not; it is possible, too, that the Pueblo people were driven away by invading tribes. Their civilization—it can rightly be called that, I think, on the evidence of architecture alone—did not die. Rather it moved southward, like a fragile drift on the Rio Grande, to the edge of the arboreal desert. It remains a vital element in the cultural composite of the Southwest, a unique synthesis of the contemporary, the historical, and the prehistoric.

Marsh Marigolds, Maroon Bells

South Colony Lakes Creek

There were then waves of migration. The plain at the base
of the mountains bloomed with clusters of encampments,
rang with the clamor of intermittent war, was marked forever with
the routes of trade, and inherent in this motion, as yet
indigenous, was a prophetic shadow on the grass, a wind in
advance of change, change absolute and unimaginable. The
Kiowa remember that they hunted antelope in the vicinity of
Bent's Fort, that they had hunted there long before the
establishment of a trading post; they were but one of many
nomadic peoples who ventured there time and again, moving
on, and on. But there were those who remained. The first white
men, the conquistadores and voyageurs, came on errands
of discovery and commerce, recording their experience of the
land. They drew the wilderness within the purview of history.
In the wake of the plainsmen and the mountain men there sprang
up the monuments of the modern age, forts, settlements, cities.
Gold was discovered in Colorado in 1858, and the camps of
Fairplay, Boulder, Gold Hill—and how many others like
them?—came tumultuously to be, where an hour before there
had been only the dark tangle of the wilderness.

Chasm Falls, Rocky Mountain National Park

Colorado was admitted to statehood on 1 August 1876, the centenary of the Declaration of Independence, and it is called, therefore appropriately, the Centennial State. Eighteen hundred and seventy-six was also the year in which the World's Fair was held at Philadelphia and Lt. Col. George Armstrong Custer was slain in the Battle of the Little Bighorn. It was a crucial time for America—and for the American West, especially. For the West was newly won.

Beyond this, there are the appearance and reality of the landscape. The landscape of Colorado is very nearly incomparable.

Bear Creek, Uncompahgre National Forest

ONCE IN the late spring I walked on the bank of Blue River. There is something in the name; it is the bluest water that I have ever seen. It shone in its channel like a flame. The sky was very pale in comparison, and yet the sky was of a deeper shade than the columbine in the meadow. There is blue, too, in the farthest shadows on the slopes. This morning I looked down from the rim of a deep canyon, and I saw that the air below me was visible—and blue.

Blue River

Trapper Lake, White River, Flat Tops

Blue Columbine

Summer

BLUE COLUMBINE along a stream high in the San Juans: an equation of blues—values, essences, implications of blue. And against the white water of a fall, such flowers achieve perfect relief, a precise clarity of color and form, an edge or system of edges, exquisitely sharp. Here is the converse of the white gem set upon blue velvet.

HERE AND there are glacial erratics, the remnants of an age in which man has only a distant and evolutionary part; his experience of it lies on the other side of human genesis. They are strange sentinels, remarking simply the interim between one Ice Age and another.

Mount Zirkel

Blazing Star

Grasslands, North Park

North Park, Rawah Range

NOTHING so much as distance informs this landscape. Every object within the range of vision has definition within the element of distance, and there only. This flower, that tree, and the mountain beyond; the eye succeeds from here to infinity. Here is the vision realized in depth. To see this landscape is to believe it; for it is exclusively possible to the eye.

ONCE the intermontane meadows rang with the voices of Indians and mountain men, carrying on the first commerce of the West. At such places I have seen in my mind's eye the camps gleaming in the early light, a thin blue smoke rising over the valley. There are horses about, hunting horses, half wild like the men who ride them, equal in their blood to the wilderness.

Hermosa Cliffs

THERE are said to be some 700 ghost towns in Colorado, founded upon the promise of silver and gold in the earth. Only for a few was the promise redeemed, and only for a fleeting moment. But the towns are there, many of them strangely intact in their skeletons. A grand story of the human spirit is told in their names: Cache Creek, Granite, Independence, Empire.

St. Elmo

Cripple Creek

THERE ARE houses that are regal ghosts. They are the vestiges of an older, more congenial age; so it seems. And yet they are surely the settings of an imperial restlessness. In the mountain towns they stand in curious relation to the backdrop of wooded slopes and the bright, ore-stained escarpments of the earth.

I have seen aged people on the streets of such towns. They have a remarkable possession of themselves, I believe, a sense of place that is nearly lost upon us whose minds are fixed upon the immediate world. One cold, clear morning on a boardwalk I saw an old, blue-eyed woman in a bonnet. I tipped her a nod, and she smiled, and we went upon our separate ways. But in her glance, in a second, I had seen something like mischief and delight—and a composure that still has a hold upon me. It was as if she had said to me, ''Oh, I can tell you a story, and you can live well within it.''

Central City

Georgetown

I REMEMBER a sunlit brake in the Park Range, carpeted with paintbrush and lupine. There were grasses, too, of shades that were scarcely distinguishable, one from another. I could see the sky through the trees in the late morning, shimmering on the high edge of August. And all at once I had the sense of that place, one sense in which every detail of the setting seemed to coalesce and converge upon me. There were a thousand things in my hearing, now that I think of it. But at the time, in view of everything there, they were constrained into the one sound of the wind.

Iris and Paintbrush

YES, the Garden of the Gods. But this is surely the work of the old, obscure deities which persist only in the moaning winds of Mesa Verde, the makers of form and substance in the earth, of music and motion, light and delight, those for whom Creation was an idea of stone monoliths in the sand, mountains in the continent, planets in the void.

Garden of the Gods

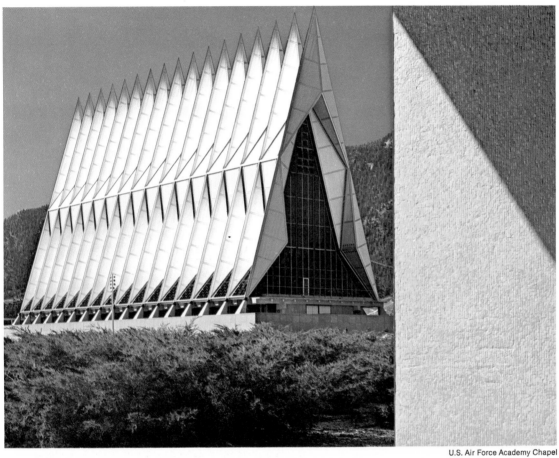

U.S. Air Force Academy Chapel

Cave of the Winds

THE OPENING of the West is in some real measure the story of railroads. The Denver & Rio Grande Railroad succeeded in the great negotiation of La Veta Pass in 1877, once and for all. The empty cars were unhitched and left behind, and another locomotive was added in their stead. The train crept upward along an average grade of 211 feet per mile for a distance of nearly twenty-two miles.

Denver

Royal Gorge, Arkansas River

Spinach Fields, San Luis Valley

Volcanic Dike, West Spanish Peak

A BLACK spine of rock lies like a great snake on the hills, as
if to verify an ancient conflagration, a remote and planetary
fire. It turns in the angles of vision; it is one thing from this point
of view, another from that. Such transformations are everywhere
about: pinnacles and wells and winding walls, seriform
seams in the earth.

Great Sand Dunes National Monument

40 COLORADO

THERE ARE great dunes in the San Luis Valley. In their softer shapes, they seem to oppose the mountains in a sense, as if they were predicated upon some vagrant principle of Creation, remote from that which informs the Cordilleras. They are hugely fluent in their definitions, and they are massive, not in the manner of mountains, but as waves in the ocean are massive. And they bear a strange and distinct relation to light, to the hours of the day and night. They seem at once to absorb and reflect all radiances of the sun and moon. Always they are peculiarly illumined, and so they make for grand illusions.

San Luis Valley

Bridal Veil Falls

THERE IS a legend which has it that the mountains were conjured up from the depths of a dark, primordial sea. Water touches a holiness to the mind and sight. Indeed it is appropriate to believe in the legend; such beliefs are integral to the soul.

Only water, in its pure, persistent life, is equal to the mountain.

The river is a ribbon of light at the bottom of a dark gorge—and a line drawing of geologic time. At noon, in a frame of dark growth, I have come upon a waterfall in the mountains and seen in it the first flare of the first dawn.

WHEN the season turns, and the earth becomes warm, bright colors appear on the land. Here and there green is predominant. The Spanish priest Escalante was the first European to see the cliff dwellings at Mesa Verde, which name he gave to the region when he came across the Mancos River in 1776.

Cliff Palace, Mesa Verde National Park

Square Tower, Mesa Verde National Park

Monument Canyon, ▶
Colorado National Monument

Mug House, Wetherill Mesa

Green River, Dinosaur National Monument

WESTWARD from the Continental Divide the Cordilleran
highlands dominate these latitudes. There is nothing like the
vast reaches of the Great Plains—only a long succession of
valleys, ridges, and summits—until you come upon the sea.
But in the interim distance there is such variety to the earth
that you can be a lifetime in imagining it.

Dinosaur National Monument

Cinnamon Pass, San Juan Mountains

Petrified Redwood

50 COLORADO

Bristlecone Pine

THE BRISTLECONES are the thorns of the ancient earth. And
they are vital. It is that, the impulse of life in them, that sets
them apart from other wonders, I believe. There have been
moments, a few, in which, by means of some extraordinary act
of the imagination, I came suddenly upon a full awareness of
the life force within me, intensely conscious of my being alive, of
sharing in the irresistible continuum of life itself. And those
moments have been as much of immortality as I can
comprehend. Such moments are concentrated in these trees,
and they have neither a beginning nor an end in time.

Limber Pines, Rocky Mountain National Park

IN 1893 Frederick Jackson Turner published his thesis entitled "The Significance of the Frontier in American History." In it he set forth the idea that the character of the wilderness itself encouraged a recurrent social revolution on each successive frontier of the westward movement, resulting in a freer, more self-sufficient society—and therefore a stronger, more definitive expression of the democratic faith. Those who were equal to the wilderness were necessarily hardier and more independent than those who were not. They personified the ideal of the frontiersman, the individual, the American.

Yes, surely such an idea is intrinsic in the relationship between man and the landscape of the American West.

Hoosier Pass, South Platte River

IT BEGINS to rain on the slopes—gently, a mere, dark transformation of the air, a squall moving diagonally down upon the highland meadows. It seems preceded by a shadow—not quite a shadow, but a vibrant gleaming of the wind, a small, bright turbulence like the rustling of leaves on the autumn earth. I hold my breath to see the rain overtake a field of clover and fireweed.

Grand Mesa

Longs Peak

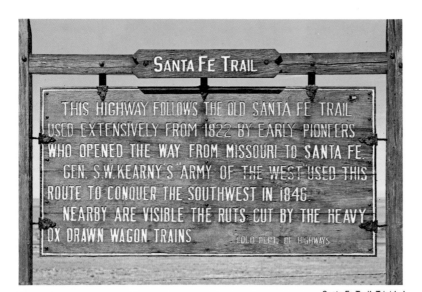

Santa Fe Trail, Trinidad

Trail Ridge Road

AMONG MY close friends is a descendant of "Uncle Dick"
Wootton. This legendary forebear, my friend tells me, built
a road over Raton Pass and collected tolls, now and then at
gunpoint. He was a man of many parts. Perhaps his most
remarkable feat was accomplished during the gold rush to
California. He started in New Mexico with 9,000 sheep; and he
delivered 8,900 of them safely to Sacramento. He established
a buffalo farm near Pueblo and opened the first saloon and
general store in Denver. And he sang bawdy songs on the
Santa Fe Trail; so says my friend.

Granite Pedestal, Rocky Mountain National Park

Saxifrage and Sandwort

Molas Lake, San Juan Mountains

THERE ARE strange formations in the canyons of the Front
Range. There are forms that seem to describe the remote
possibilities of Creation. Here and there are monoliths
against the sky. They seem to stand in peculiar relation to time,
or in no relation whatsoever, as if eternity were their element.

Bear Lake, Rocky Mountain National Park

Fall

THERE ARE meadows of buckwheat and grasses on the lower slopes. I walked for a long time one day and lay down in a meadow to sleep. Later, when I awoke, I looked through a bunch of buckwheat at the sky. At point-blank range, I noticed for the first time that buckwheat grows in horizontal layers. On a miniature scale it bears a resemblance to the thorn tree of Africa.

South Park, Mosquito and Tenmile Ranges

EVERYWHERE, at times, the landscape is in motion. There is a glittering upon it, an incessant, visible rhythm to the life of the earth. The mountains approach and recede in mists, clouds move across the sky, trailing their shadows on the grasses, and there is a constant vibration on the trees. Milkweed pods, with their long filaments flaring, are like dancing dolls.

Wheat Field

Milkweed Pods

Foxtail Barley

Fall River, Mummy Range

THE EASTERN slope of the Rockies is a range upon which
great herds of buffalo moved in numberless processions. "The
country was one robe," said someone who was there. No one,
of course, knows how many of these animals inhabited the whole
expanse of the Great Plains at any one time; a reasonable,
perhaps conservative, guess is thirty million. Nathaniel Langford,
later the first superintendent of Yellowstone National Park,
wrote of sighting a herd near the Cheyenne River in 1862:
". . . we judged the herd to be 5 or 6 (some said 8 or 10) miles
wide, and the herd was more than an hour passing us at a
gallop . . . I have no doubt that there were one million
buffaloes in that herd."

There were pronghorns, too. The Kiowa remember having
hunted antelope on foot and with clubs in the vicinity of
Bent's Fort.

Now there are farms on the slope. Here and there are fields
of sorghum, deep in the color of rust. Perhaps, in some rare,
organic equation, it is the blood of the buffalo.

Sorghum Fields

Silverton

Leadville and Mount Massive

IN THE abandoned mines of Colorado there is evidence of man's tentative relation to, and tenure in, the landscape of the Rocky Mountains. They remark a curiously dormant, nearly negligible tension between time and timelessness. They seem the most immediate and vulnerable aberrations of the soil. And yet they are endowed with a kind of organic significance, measuring as they do the extension of human history to the wilderness. There is an aesthetic aspect to this equation. The windows of ruins are often frames in which a particular view of the natural world is informed with symmetry, selection, and precision.

IN AUTUMN there is a rich glaze on the high, wooded slopes. The aspen leaves, especially, make a fine, brilliant carpet on the dark, damp earth. At a distance they are pools of light, and their brilliance is of a low, even intensity. But as you approach, various orders of color and shape emerge upon them, patterns within patterns, forms and facets without end.

HAWKS SAIL in circles above the foothills. In autumn there is a haze on the skyline. You look into the distance for a long time, wondering if it is rain that you see. Or is it something else, an apparent sheen upon the near side of infinity, a pale wash like rain?

La Veta Pass, Sangre de Cristo Range

Pikes Peak

◄ Snowmass Canyon

THE ALPINE rangelands are the great hollows of the Rockies, deeply informed with colors that have no true reflections elsewhere in the world. Weather inheres in them. You see them from high above, and you sense that they exist in an element that is peculiarly their own, a spatial dimension that you perceive but do not inhabit. And when you descend into them you feel in your blood a strange and perfect exhilaration. Shadows move about you on the grain, and eagles describe the cold currents of the sky.

Aspen Trees, Grand Mesa

Elk Mountains

Alpine Fir, Cottonwood Pass

Limber Pines, Trail Ridge Road

THERE IS in my memory an autumn evening in which the full moon rides in the farthest reaches of the night sky. Here, below, there is a lake, fringed with high, black growth. The track of the moon in the water is a bright line, full of low, shimmering brilliance. A vague, planetary agitation bears upon it, a mysterious tension of the tides. It is forever whole, and forever breaking apart.

Snowmass Canyon

Sangre de Cristo Range

Winter

IN 1851, six families settled at the center of the Sangre de Cristo Grant, just north of the present town of San Luis. They were of Spanish descent, and they served to extend the great cultural vitality of New Spain northward. They built their houses, which faced inward upon a plaza, to form a kind of wall for protection. On the outer perimeter there were no doors or windows. This idea of the walled enclosure, in which the life's blood is centered, must be one of the oldest strategies known to man.

THE COLD is a splintering of planes. Splinters of light inform
the winter dawn and dusk, glance at water and glacial lees. The
sky is splintered at the brittle limbs of a tree, and here and
there in the snowfields are thin radial shadows at the drifts,
splinters of long grass and grain.

THE VISTAS are everywhere and unending. The long blue skyline reaches higher, farther into space than yesterday—in view of other landscapes you thought possible. And the middle distances penetrate beyond your reckoning. Here, all lines of sight are trained upon infinity. There are consequent reactions to such perceptions as these, a stirring of the mind and of the blood. I think: Here is my imagination realized to its whole potential. Nothing of what I behold is lost upon me here; the wilderness fulfills my sphere of instinct, and I am as intensely alive as I ever was or will be.

Sierra Blanca

WILLIAM BENT, who in partnership with his brothers and Ceran St. Vrain founded Bent's Fort, married Owl Woman, the daughter of the Cheyenne shaman White Thunder. Owl Woman died in childbirth, and William married her sister, Yellow Woman. Charles Bent, who married Kit Carson's sister-in-law, Inezita Jaramillo, was appointed first territorial governor of New Mexico. Here is a concentrated network of frontier nobility, and here the establishment of a remarkable complex—cultural, social, military, and mercantile: an American dynasty.

San Luis Valley

Sangre de Cristo Range

THE GREAT SPINE of the continent falls away eastward to vast reaches of level land. A semiarid, treeless expanse extends to infinity. There is sparse, brittle growth, there a bit of cactus, and there the bleached bones of a cow. Somehow these effects have no influence upon the principle of immense, inviolate space. The empty sky is precisely equal to the empty land. It is a conjugation of great strengths.

Wilson Peaks

Animas River, West Needles Range

Grizzly Peak, San Juan Mountains

West Needles Range, San Juan Mountains

AT ASPEN or Vail—any one of a hundred places—in winter, the skiers glide on the long slopes, describing an intricate tracery on the snowfields. I love to see them; it seems an order of motion that proceeds from basic dimensions of artistry and grace. Such speed and fluency seem appropriate to soaring birds, in which creatures such motion is natural. In man it is artistic.

Aspen

COTTONWOODS seem especially indigenous to the peneplains
of the Rockies. More than other trees they reflect the seasonal
character of the landscape in the most various intensities of
color and form. They are the true delineations of change; they
remark the seasons entirely in themselves, and you need have
no other reference to the time of year.

In January you catch sight of cottonwoods in a cluster,
their branches frosted in the most intricate image of winter, a
frozen filigree beyond which no focus is possible in the
range of vision.

Crestone Peak, Sangre de Cristo Range

Sneffels Range

Spring

AN AGED farmer takes my hand in greeting. And "takes" is the right word; there is strength and possession in his grasp. "I am glad," he says, simply, and there can be no doubt that he is glad. This is no easy formula for him; he doesn't waste words.

He presents his son to me, and his grandson. The young man has the old man's hands, and the boy will have them in time, provided that he touches them to the land. But there are alternative destinies; I see them in the boy's eyes. We think about them in our separate ways.

Abandoned Farm

Telluride

A CHILD who is born in the mountains has them forever in his mind. They bear upon the mind like a magnet. I have seen evidence of this in my own racial experience. The Kiowa, when they entered upon the Great Plains, were a long time—many generations—in holding the mountains in their view. They kept within the rain shadow of the Rockies, following the track of the winterbound sun southward to the rolling plains. And when their long journey came to an end, there were low, isolated mountains in their view.

Snowmass Mountain

ONCE AMONG the mountains I flew alone in a light plane. I had
the sense that I was entering into a great maze of the earth, in
which the force of gravity was severe, broken, and erratic. The
mountains exerted a crucial, irresistible force upon the air, and I
was caught up in an element that I could not have imagined.
I became suddenly conscious of the dark immensities on every
side, and of the deep, turbulent vortex in which I was suspended
by means of a fragile and quaking machine. Never before—and
not since—have I known such a feeling of buoyancy in my
mind and body. It was as if the earth had let go of me and I had
succeeded to some perfect equilibrium in and of the sky.

Mounts Hagerman and Snowmass, Elk Mountains

Saxifrage

Maroon Bells-Snowmass Wilderness

Spring Beauty and Forget-me-nots, Mount Evans

Roaring Fork Canyon

WEATHER adheres to the top of the continent. You see at the distant summits a gathering of clouds from which there emanates a dark, roiling mist, run through with flashes of light. And when you hear it, thunder rolls upon the slopes for a long time, longer than you expect, longer at last than you believe. But something of your perception is sustained there at the center of the storm, a shade beyond your belief.

San Juan Mountains from Cimarron Peak

Canyon Creek, Ouray

Sneffels Creek, San Juan Mountains

Hidden Valley Cascade, Rocky Mountain National Park

IN LATE spring buttercups ring the lakes of the high country. From a distance they create a field of color in the eye, a vague circle, or a ribbon that has fallen down to make a bright and indefinite pattern on the land. They trace the water's edge and give to it a hard and brilliant relief. The eye can integrate such juxtapositions; they suggest the first idea of cartography in the mind.

On closer view there are white and blue and sand-colored stones among the bells and buttercups. There is at once an elaboration and a disintegration of color, confusion in the best sense. It is not easy to see clearly into the physical world, but it is eminently worthwhile to try. I am told by an old Indian that it is good for the eye to behold a sky-blue stone.

Fireweed

Buttercups

Maroon Creek, White River National Forest

Aspen Reflections, Grand Mesa

Arkansas Valley, Sawatch Range

SUDDENLY, when you have been looking into the bright light—the shattered reflection of the sun in a stream, the facets of a frozen drift—and raise your eyes, you see someone approaching on the path, descending upon you from the wall of the wood. He is mysterious, for he is indistinct, a silhouette fringed with red and orange light. In his passage, some quality of the wilderness adheres to him. He nods to you and continues on his way.

Owl Creek Pass

IN COLORADO there is a certain grandeur in the formation of clouds, a full-blown aspect that I have not seen in other landscapes. There especially do the clouds roil and billow and sail in motion so slow as to be nearly indiscernible. They are often very sharp in their definition, and three-dimensional. They are massive, like the mountains to which they adhere, and they appear to have the same depth and density. They range in the hold of the mountains and the plain, rolling close upon the curve of the earth, downward from the Continental Divide.

Mountain Anemone

HERE you perceive a special character in the seasons. Spring and summer achieve a deeper, farther expression of themselves; autumn is not elsewhere so closely involved in the turning of the earth; and winter is definitive. Nor are the seasons entirely sequential on the slopes of the Rockies, but there are transitions that are seasons in themselves, wonderfully various and perceptible. These are mutations of the earth and air, and their images are whole and endlessly recurrent: the gathering of a storm at a distant ridge, a scattering of snowmelts in a stream, a reflection of quaking aspens upon water, a shadow moving across dunes.

Lone Eagle Peak, Front Range